Subology:

A Substitute Teacher's Guide

to Successful Days

By Karen Bradford

Illustrated by
Leland Howard Johnson

authorHOUSE®

AuthorHouse™
1663 Liberty Drive, Suite 200
Bloomington, IN 47403
www.authorhouse.com
Phone: 1-800-839-8640

First published by AuthorHouse 4/3/2009

ISBN: 978-1-4389-0908-0 (sc)

Library of Congress Control Number: 2008910773

*Printed in the United States of America
Bloomington, Indiana*

This book is printed on acid-free paper.

Contents

INTRODUCTION

I remember being very nervous my first few days of teaching in a classroom. My palms were sweaty, my voice quavered, and my heart was pounding in my chest. I wanted to succeed and be a great teacher, but I was afraid that I would fail because I did not have any teaching experience.

I got through the first few days without incident. I carried my lesson plan around with me and checked it frequently so that I would not forget to do everything on it. I praised the students when they gave a correct answer and encouraged them to try again when they were wrong. I stood in front of the class so everyone could see me, spoke loudly so they could hear me, wrote legibly on the chalk board, so they could follow along and gave my best explanations of the lessons. Luckily, I didn't have any major behavior problems from the students. I didn't feel that I was doing a bad job, but I knew I had a lot to learn to become a better teacher.

The more time I spent in the classroom, the more I learned. I received valuable advice from my fellow teachers. They gave me ideas on how to present lesson plans, ways to keep the students engaged in the lesson and advice on how to be in control of the classroom. Their support encouraged me. Their guidance allowed me to form strategies that worked best for me.

It is my desire to pass along the knowledge I acquired from my experiences of teaching Spanish in two New York City Catholic Schools, being a teacher's assistant and substitute teacher in Department of Defense schools in Mannheim, Germany, and substitute teaching in Dayton and Columbus Public Schools in Ohio.

This guide is designed to give the substitute teacher advice on events that occur during a typical school day. This information includes important items to bring, ideas on how to present the lesson, and ways to maintain order in the classroom. While no method is guaranteed to work every time in every classroom situation, this guide provides practical and useful information that can be easily used and adapted in the classroom. My hope is that future substitute teachers will use the advice in this guide to formulate their own strategies so they may have many successful days in the classroom.

1

TRAITS OF A GREAT
SUBSTITUTE TEACHER

Thinking back to when I was in school, I remember two kinds of substitute teachers. Bad substitutes struck fear into our little hearts and made us groan the moment we saw them. They would fill our minds with threats of physical harm for less-than-perfect behavior. They were disorganized, unsure of themselves, and unable to keep the class in order. Most would resort to yelling and screaming in an attempt to intimidate us and keep us behaving properly.

On the other hand, there were good substitutes we loved to see standing in the classroom. We knew we would have a good day with them because they respected us and in turn we respected them. They were self-confident, kept everything under control, and successfully instructed us in our daily lessons. They did their best, and we enjoyed having them in our class for that day.

As a substitute teacher:
▶ Be confident in yourself and your work. The more confidence you have in yourself and who you are, the more the students will pick up on that and respect you.
▶ Be a positive role model. Students learn as much from you as they learn from the textbooks. They see how you present yourself, how you take care of yourself, and that you want to do your best. They will be able to see that you care for them and want them to do their best.

▶Have a positive attitude. Believe that you will do a great job, and you will.

▶Do your best. No one expects you to be perfect. Learn from what works and what doesn't.

▶Be patient with yourself. Remember, becoming great at anything takes time.

▶Use good body language. Stand up straight. Hold your shoulders back. Stand tall. Walk confidently.

▶Don't be afraid of making a mistake. We are all human and we all make mistakes. The students will find you more human and honorable if you admit to your mistake and take steps to correct it than if you lie and try to cover it up.

▶Know what you know and be willing to learn more. Be willing to learn something new every day and you will expand your knowledge. You do not have to know the answers to everything. If there is a question that you don't know how to answer, admit it. But take every possible step to find the answer with the class.

▶Hold your ground and stick to the rules and decisions you make. By treating everyone by the same rules, there is no confusion. By sticking to the decisions you make, you won't be manipulated by the students into doing things you know are not wise or not what the teacher wants.

▶ Use your common sense. If students ask you to do something that doesn't sound right, it probably isn't. If they say their regular teacher lets them go to the gym instead of staying in class, tell them they will have to tough it out in class for that day and wait until their teacher comes back.

▶ You are there to teach the students not to become their best friend. If a student says he or she doesn't like you, it is not your mission to get that student to change his or her mind. It is your mission to teach and help that student with the assignments for the day.

The impression you leave is one that will last forever. It takes only one time for a student to meet you, see the light that shines within you, and be forever inspired by you to do his or her best. It takes only a few encouraging words to get students to do the best they can do. It takes only a little patience to help a student understand something that is difficult. Make every effort to do the best job you can do and leave a great impression.

2

BEFORE YOU ENTER A CLASSROOM

Depending on your location and your preferences, you may be able to apply to public or private school systems. The educational requirements, required experience, your responsibilities, and the benefits you will receive as a substitute differ in every school system. Requirements may range from a high school diploma to a teaching certificate. A school system may ask that substitutes have extensive previous classroom experience or none at all.

Research the school system(s) you are interested in to find out the requirements, benefits offered, and responsibilities required of a substitute teacher to determine in which one you want to work.

Once you have decided in which school system you want to teach:
- ▶Contact the local board of education for public schools or the main office of the

private school of your choice to obtain information on the application process.

► Fill out an application.

► Get fingerprinted and have a background check completed. By law, most school systems require potential employees be fingerprinted and have a background check completed to ensure that they do not have criminal records or are a threat to students. There could possibly be a fee for the cost of the fingerprinting and background check.

► Other requirements may include:

　► An official copy of your high school or university transcript

　► Health tests to ensure that you are in good health

　► Essay questions to demonstrate your writing skills and philosophy about teaching

Normally, after you submit your application with all the required documents, there will be a short waiting period to review your application and complete the background check. The school system will notify you when you have been cleared to substitute.

3

ASSEMBLING YOUR GREATEST RESOURCE
THE JUST-IN-CASE BAG

While waiting for the application to be processed, you can put together your greatest resource, the Just-In-Case Bag. The articles you put in your bag can come from home, be purchased in discount stores and teachers supply stores or borrowed from the public library. Use these items just in case you want to reward the students for doing a great job or just in case the students finish the assignment early or just in case the regular teacher did not leave lesson plans.

Useful items to include in the Just-in-Case Bag:

Attention-getting signal	Music CD
Bell/Whistle	Prizes/Rewards
Emergency Lesson Plan	Storybook
Games	Supplies
Learning activity books	Timer
Movie	Watch

▶ **Attention-getting signal**

An audio or visual signal that gets the attention of the entire class can be helpful when teaching students. The signal can be used to quiet the students down and have them focus their attention on you anytime the noise level in the classroom is getting too high or their behavior is starting to get out of hand.

Upon giving the signal, the students are to "freeze", meaning that they are to stop talking, stop doing whatever they are doing, and focus their attention on you. Once everyone is quiet and looking at you, give them directions, let them know that they need to quiet down or behave in a more appropriate manner.

One example of an attention-getting signal is a signal sentence. The signal sentence should be one that gets the attention of the students and should be used only for that purpose.

A possible signal sentence is, *"If you can hear the sound of my voice, clap once."*

The students are to clap once after hearing your signal sentence. Clap with them.

If there are students who did not hear the signal sentence and are still talking or moving about the room, say, *"If you can hear the sound of my voice, clap twice."*

Clap twice with them. By the end of the second clap, the students need to be quiet, listening, and looking at you.

Another example of an attention-getting signal is turning the classroom lights off. Explain to the students that when the lights go off they are to stop talking and moving around and wait for your directions. For younger students, you can tell them that they are robots and when the lights go off, their batteries have run out of power and therefore they no longer can talk or walk around. The only way they can get their power back is to look at you and listen to your directions.

Once you have the attention of the class, direct them as needed.

Use an attention-getting signal that is easily identified by the students. Show and explain it to them in the beginning of class. Practice it a few times so that they understand what they have to do when they hear or see it.

▶ **Bell/Whistle**

If your students have outdoor recess, a noisemaker, like a bell or whistle, will help you round them up when it is time to go inside. Tell the students what noisemaker you have so that they will know what to listen for. Tell them that when you blow the whistle or ring the bell, they are to stop playing and get in line to go inside.

▶**Emergency Lesson Plan**

Some teachers may not be able to leave a lesson plan because they do not anticipate their absence and are unable to go to the school to prepare a lesson for you. It is a good idea to be prepared with something to get the students working and occupied while you plan out the day.

The emergency lesson plan can be a learning activity book page, subject-specific workbook page, small art project, experiment or any learning activity you can create. Pass out the necessary materials or worksheet pages, explain the activity to the class, do an example together, and then let them finish the rest. While the students are working on the lesson, use the time to create a lesson plan for the rest the day.

Make sure the emergency lesson plan is appropriate for the grade level and subject you are teaching. Keep the instructions, materials and/or set of worksheets in your bag.

▶ Games

Games are a fun way to take a quick learning break or fill extra time at the end of a class. It is good to know a few games to play that involve the entire class. School supply stores have books you can buy filled with games you can play in the classroom. You can also find game ideas on the internet. Type "classroom games" into your favorite search engine and you will have several websites to visit.

▶ Learning activity books and subject-specific workbooks

Learning activity books and subject-specific workbooks are a fun way to keep your students working quietly and learning if they have finished their work early and need something to do to keep them occupied. They can also be used as your emergency lesson plan.

Learning activity books are filled with fun worksheets and teaching ideas.

They come in a variety of lessons and grade levels and can contain coloring book pages, crossword puzzles, word searches, brainteasers, art projects, and experiments.

Subject-specific workbooks have exercises that deal with one subject area, for example Mathematics. They come in all grade levels and contain a variety of lessons. If you have a favorite subject area and are interested in substitute teaching in only that area, they may be a good investment for you.

Learning activities books and subject specific workbooks can be purchased in discount stores, bookstores, or school supply stores. Purchase the books you think the students will find most interesting or that seem to have many subjects and themes.

You may also find a variety of free printable learning activities and subject specific worksheets on the internet. Type in "lesson plans" into your favorite search engine and you will have many websites to visit.

Make enough copies of the page(s) you want to use for an entire class before you go into the classroom. Most schools will allow you to use the copier, but just in case it is broken, make a set before hand.

► **Movie (G-rated), educational video, or cartoon**

This item can be used as a reward when the students have worked hard and finished their work early and there is still time left at the end of the day or class. A video may also be used to help keep the students' attention if the teacher did not leave any lesson plans, and you need time to plan out the day.

Most classrooms have a TV and DVD/ VCR player. If not, you may be able to sign them out for the day from the school's library. Also, if you do not have a video, you may be able to borrow an appropriate one for your class from the school's library.

If you bring in your own video, it is a good idea to get the school's administration to approve it before showing it to a class.

Warning: Some videos may only be licensed for viewing privately at home. Check the video you bring in for a warning label prohibiting public viewing. Schools can be fined if these videos are shown in classrooms.

▶ Music CD

Music in the classroom can be used to energize, motivate, calm, or relax students. There are a variety of CDs that you can take into the classroom to accomplish these different goals.

For younger students, sing-along CDs have songs that the students may already know or the songs may be simple enough that you can teach the students in a few minutes. Put motions to the words to really get the students involved in the song.

Exercise CDs are a fun way to get the students moving. They will have the students stretching, walking, or dancing to the directions sung out by the singer(s).

There are also CDs of popular fables, fairy tales, and nursery rhymes. You can choose students to act out the story in front of the class.

The class can sing along together when you need a break from what you are doing, when there is group/circle time, to energize students when they are sluggish or to burn off excess energy.

Older students may enjoy listening to music in different languages. This is especially effective if you are teaching a language class and have music in that particular language. Challenge the students by having them listen and try to understand what the song is about and/or interpret what they hear. This also gives them a look into a different culture through their music.

Classical music was played when I was in high school by the Physics teacher on test days to relax the students. Most of the students agreed that it did help them concentrate and do better on the tests. Give it a try if your students have a test to take or while they are working on assignments.

Be sure to only play the music when the students are working and not while you are teaching or explaining the assignment.

Be sure to get the school's administration to approve any music CDs you plan on using in the classroom.

▶ **Prizes/Rewards**

When the students you are teaching have been well behaved and completed all their assignments or you want to thank them for working hard, a reward may be in order. Candy, shiny new pencils, and colorful character stickers are examples of inexpensive rewards that students love to work for, especially candy. Pencils and stickers are good for the students who cannot or do not like to eat candy.

▶ **Storybook**

If you find you have finished the lesson early and need to fill time, you can read a story out loud. If you don't have a storybook, borrow one from the public library in your area. To help with your book selection, some public libraries have lists of new or popular juvenile books arranged by grade level or age. Many teachers have storybooks in their room or you can borrow them from the school's library.

It is a good idea to get approval for your storybook from the school's administration if it is one you brought to the school.

►**Supplies - paper, pens, pencils, chalk, crayons, markers, highlighters, paperclips, stapler**

Throughout the day, you will need to make notes to yourself and the teacher or write information on the chalkboard. Most teachers have supplies available to you in their desk. Some may hide them from their students, and inadvertently, you. Take your own supplies so you are sure to have them.

►**Timer**

You may have an activity that needs to be timed, for example, taking a quiz. To ensure that the students get the exact amount of time promised and to signal them when time is up, a timer with a buzzer is a great alarm to have. When time is up, the timer lets the class know it is time to change activities.

▶ **Watch**

This time telling device will keep you on schedule. Be sure to have one when you go outside for recess so you know when to go back in or just in case the clock in your room doesn't work.

You need only a few items and ideas in your Just-In-Case Bag to keep your class flowing harmoniously, keep your students busy, or help you just in case you need an extra activity. How many items you take and which ones is up to you. Add new items that you find useful to your Just-In-Case Bag and eliminate the ones you do not use.

4

ACCEPTING THE ASSIGNMENT
THAT IS RIGHT FOR YOU

The fun begins after your application packet has been processed and you have been informed that you may start accepting assignments. The greatest advantage to being a substitute teacher is the freedom of choosing assignments. The freedom to choose the days you want to work, the grade level, the subject, the school, and even the teacher you want to substitute for are benefits that all substitutes enjoy.

The school system may notify you of open assignments either by someone calling you directly from the school or by an automated message system. Depending on the size of the school system, there may be many assignments from which to choose.

Think about the following to help you select an assignment:

- ▶ **The type of school** - elementary, middle school, or high school
- ▶ **The grade level of the students** - 1st, 2nd, 3rd, etc.
- ▶ **The subject area** - Math, Science, Art, etc.
- ▶ **The school** - if you have a specific school you want to teach in or whether you are willing to work in many different schools
- ▶ **The length of the assignment** - one day, three days, one week

Select assignments that you feel you will succeed in teaching. If you do not have any previous experience teaching students, pick the grade level to which you can best relate, the subject area in which you are most knowledgeable and a school whose location you are familiar.

Write down all the information given after you have selected and accepted an assignment:

- ▶ The teacher's name
- ▶ The school
- ▶ The grade level or subject

►The date and how many days you are needed

►The arrival time

Once you gain experience and are comfortable being in a classroom, experiment with different types of assignments. Try a different grade level, subject or school. See what it is like to be in a kindergarten class for a day if you normally substitute in high school. Try being the art or music teacher if you only substitute for regular classroom teachers. You may find your interests lie in something you never considered.

5

ARRIVAL AT THE SCHOOL – WHERE TO GO, WHAT TO DO

Walking into an unfamiliar school building can be overwhelming. Schools are always charged with a lot of energy before the beginning of the school day as teachers and other staff move about, finalizing their plans for the day. The first challenge of the day may be finding the main office among the twists and turns of the hallways.

The arrival time you are given is usually the same time the regular teachers are required to report to school. It is better to arrive 10 to 15 minutes earlier than the given arrival time. This extra time can mean the difference between you running around trying to get the lesson ready or you calmly greeting your students when they enter the classroom.

Report to the main office upon arrival at the school. Once there, the office staff will help you start your day off right. This is your opportunity to ask the main office staff any questions you may have.

Be sure to:

▶ Sign in and/or pick up a key to the classroom, if required.

▶ Ask what the school's policy is on hall, library, restroom, and clinic passes.

▶ Request a copy of the teacher and student handbooks. They contain detailed information on the school's policies. You can refer to them if you have a question once you are in your classroom.

▶ Find out whether there will be any changes to the normal daily schedule, such as a fire or tornado drill or a school assembly. If any of these events are scheduled during the day, find out where you will need to go, what you will need to do, and at what time it is scheduled to happen.

► Some schools have telephones in the classrooms for teachers to use in emergencies. Ask whether your classroom will have one. If there is a telephone, get a copy of the school's telephone number list. Highlight the numbers you would need in case of emergency, like the main office, security office or clinic. Usually students are not allowed to use the classroom telephones. Check with the main office staff to see what the school's policy is on student usage.

► Request a copy of the school's floor plan. This will come in handy if you have to move your students to different classrooms.

► Inquire about giving after-school detention and the discipline procedure for sending a student to the principal's office. (With luck, you will never have to send anyone out, but if you do, it is good to know the school's procedure.)

▶ Pick up the "substitute teacher folder," if the school requires teachers to leave one. The substitute folder usually contains a copy of the lesson plans, a note from the teacher, a list of the rules and consequences, attendance sheets, seating chart, and a class schedule.

Any uncertainties you have can be clarified by the main office staff. Because procedures differ from school to school, it is a good idea to keep notes on each school's specific procedures.

After you have signed in, received a key for your classroom, and have answers to all of your questions, find your classroom. The first thing you want to look for is the lesson plan book.

6

LESSON PLANS – THE BLUEPRINTS FOR THE DAY

Lesson plans are the blueprints for the day. They provide you with the class schedule, the learning objectives, the lesson being studied, the materials needed, the pages covered, the assignment, and the homework.

Read over the lesson plans and determine the following:
- ▶ What will the class learn or review?
- ▶ What is the in-class assignment?
- ▶ What book(s), workbook(s), or worksheet(s)/ handout(s) are needed?
- ▶ On which pages in the book(s) or workbook(s) is the assignment?
- ▶ When is the assignment due?
- ▶ Is there a homework assignment?
- ▶ Are there any other details or notes the teacher has left to help students complete the assignment?

►Is there any information you need to tell the students or write on the chalkboard (book name, page number, etc.)?

Once you read over the lesson plans and understand what you should be doing:

►Read over the assignment and go through the exercises you are to teach to familiarize yourself with what the class will study.

►Look over the answer key. If an answer key is not available, try to answer the problems yourself. You will be able to guide the students to correctly answer the problems if you are familiar with the material and already know the answers.

►Find the teacher's manuals, books, worksheets, handouts, or other materials needed. Arrange the materials on the teacher's desk so that you will be able to use or pass them out easily and quickly. The more easily you can find what you need, the more smoothly the class will run.

►If you do not understand what the teacher is trying to accomplish or you cannot find the books, teacher's manuals, or worksheets needed, ask another teacher in the same subject or grade level for help. These teachers will be able to help you understand the lesson plan and may be able to help you find, or loan you, the materials needed.

► Some teachers may write a note to you explaining any special class routines, rules and consequences, or the names of good teacher's helpers or class clowns. The teacher's note may also give you other important information to pass on to the students.

► Check for any extra duty you may be assigned. Some schools require teachers to have extra duty either before or after school. Extra duty is any task that helps the day run smoothly or monitors the behavior of the students. For example, if the teacher you are substitute teaching for has bus duty, making sure the students get off the bus and into the school safely, you will have to do it. The main office staff or other teachers will be able to help you get to where you need to go and explain what you need to do if it is not clear.

To give you an idea of what a lesson plan may look like, the next pages provide examples of daily schedules and lesson plans from the lesson plan books from a second grade elementary school teacher, a middle school language arts teacher, and a high school Spanish teacher.

ELEMENTARY SCHOOL

In elementary school, students stay with one teacher for the majority of the day.

Daily class schedules will vary for each school and teacher for whom you substitute. The teacher may create his or her own schedule, deciding at which time and for how long to teach a subject or teachers of the same grade in the same school may have similar schedules.

The length of time spent on each subject may vary. There are also activities that the students attend outside of the classroom, such as Music or Art. A few minutes of travel time is usually incorporated into the schedule when students walk from their classroom to other rooms, to the lunch room, or outdoors.

Teachers may establish special rules or routines to keep their students behaving properly and to keep the classroom in order. Try to follow these routines as closely as possible. Younger students get used to the rules and routines of their classroom and may not adjust easily to major changes. Let the students know that you will do your best to do things the way their teacher does them but remind them that you are not the regular teacher and some things may not be exactly the same.

The schedule for Mrs. Mills' second grade class is an example of what a class schedule for a second grade teacher may look like.

Mrs. Mills' Second Grade Class Schedule

School Day - 8:30–2:30

8:30–8:40	Attendance/lunch count
8:40–9:00	Group Time
9:00–9:50	Spelling
9:50–10:10	Indoor Recess
10:10–11:10	Reading
11:15–11:45	Lunch
11:45–12:15	Recess
12:20–1:05	Art
1:10–1:50	Science
1:50–2:20	Math
2:20–2:30	Prepare to Go Home

Mrs. Mills' Lesson Plans for Tuesday, April 4

8:30-8:40   Attendance/lunch count

8:40-9:00   Group Time

Show and tell student: Sam. Question of the day: What is your favorite food?

9:00-9:50   Spelling

Introduce new spelling words on page 45 of *Spelling Is Fun*. Review words with students. Have students complete word search worksheet *Spelling is Fun* #10, and turn it in when completed. Have students write spelling words three times each on a sheet of paper to take home and study.

9:50-10:10   Indoor Recess

Board games, big building blocks, toy cars, dolls, coloring books, and crayons.

10:10-11:10   Reading

Read "Molly's New Green Coat" on pages 25–35 in *Second Grade Stories*.

11:15-11:45   Lunch

Walk students to cafeteria. Lunch.

11:45-12:15   Recess

Yellow playground equipment

12:20-1:05   Art

Room 105/Planning Period

1:10-1:50   Science

Watch *Animals of the Desert* video. Have students answer questions on the worksheet and turn in for participation points.

1:50-2:20   Math

Worksheet – Adding Two Columns of Numbers. Students are to complete the worksheet using the small building blocks to help them count. Students are to take sheets home and review with parents.

2:20-2:30   Prepare to Go Home

Students take home necessary books and papers. They get coats and backpacks from closet.

The note Mrs. Mills left for the substitute teacher:

Dear Substitute Teacher,

Thank you for filling in for me today! All teacher's manuals and worksheets for the students are in the top right-hand corner of my desk. Please put the work you collect from the students in the yellow tray on my desk.

First thing in the morning, the students come in and put their coats and backpacks in the closet. Each student has his or her own hook.

Attendance and lunch count. If the main office staff did not give you the attendance and lunch count sheets when you signed in, they are in my mailbox in the main office. Please fill them out in pencil.

Group time. After morning announcements, the students are to go to the back of the room and sit on the blue carpet. We say good morning to one another and shake hands. I pick five students to tell me something fun or exciting they did the night before or something they will do on the weekend. After that, we have show and tell.

Sam Smith is the Show and Tell student for today. He is allowed 5–7 minutes to show and tell about the toy he brought in and answer any questions the other students may have about it. When group time is finished, Sam is to put his toy on my desk. He may play with it during recess, but it is to go back on my desk until the end of the day. Please remind him to take it home.

Write the question of the day, "What is your favorite food?" on the white dry erase board. All students are to answer the question in a complete sentence, for example, "My favorite food is...."

At the end of group time, the students will sing the song "It's Time to Learn." The words to the song are in the blue folder on my desk.

Indoor recess is from 9:50 to 10:10. The students are allowed to play with the board games, big building blocks, toy cars, dolls, coloring books, and crayons. All items can be found in the "Games" cabinet on the third and fourth shelves. Please do not let students write on the chalkboard.

At 11:10, walk the students to the cafeteria for lunch. The lunchroom monitors will direct them where to go. This is also the time you should eat lunch.

Pick the students up at 11:45 from the cafeteria, and walk them outside for recess. I have recess duty today, so you must stay outside with all of the students. Students are to play on the yellow playground equipment and are <u>NOT</u> allowed to go on to the basketball courts.

After recess, walk the students to room 105 for art with Mrs. Ball. She will bring them back to our classroom when art class is finished.

Science. The Animals of the Desert video is in the "Teacher Only" cabinet on the second shelf. The TV and VCR are already hooked up.

For math time, the small blocks are in the cabinet marked "Teacher Only" on the third shelf. Please make sure the students use the blocks to help them count; they should not play with them.

At the end of the day, students are to take home the papers from their mailboxes under the windows. They get their coats and backpacks from the closet, and stand beside their desks until the bell rings. We walk to the main hallway together. Their parents or bus drivers will be there to pick them up.

Joshua Stein is a wonderful helper. He knows the classroom rules and routines and he can help you find anything you need in the classroom.

If you have any questions, Mr. Joseph, across the hall, can help you.

I hope you have a wonderful day!
Thanks again!

Mrs. Mills

MIDDLE SCHOOL AND HIGH SCHOOL

In middle school and high school, each teacher has a specific subject area that he or she teaches. Within that subject area, a teacher may teach a variety of topics. For example, a history teacher may teach American history, American government and European history.

Middle schools and high schools have several class periods during the day. Every period the students change classes and go to a different teacher and classroom to study a different subject.

Each school has its own schedule, and the length of the class periods may vary. Students are given a few minutes in between periods to move from classroom to classroom.

In the example of the middle school schedule, the school day begins at 8:25 a.m. and ends at 3:55 p.m. There are seven class periods lasting fifty-five minutes each. The students are given five minutes to change classes.

In the example of the high school schedule, the school day begins at 7:53 a.m. and ends at 2:00 p.m. There are eight class periods lasting forty-two minutes each.

<u>Middle School Day 8:25 – 3:55</u>

1st Period - 8:25 – 9:20

2nd Period - 9:25 – 10:20

3rd Period - 10:25 - 11:20

4th Period - 11:25 – 12:20

Lunch - 12:25–12:55

5th Period - 1:00–1:55

6th Period - 2:00–2:55

7th Period - 3:00–3:55

<u>High School Day   7:53 - 2:00</u>

Homeroom - 7:53 - 8:00

1st Period - 8:00–8:42

2nd Period - 8:45–9:27

3rd Period - 9:30–10:12

4th Period - 10:15–10:57

5th Period –11:00–11:42

6th Period – 11:45–12:27

7th Period – 12:30–1:12

8th Period – 1:15 – 2:00

Some schools use a block schedule, alternating half of their classes on Day "A" and the other half on Day "B." In this example, each class last an hour and a half.

Block schedule example:
Day A
1st Period - 8:00–9:30
2nd Period - 9:35–11:05
Lunch   -   11:10–11:50
3rd Period - 11:55–1:25
4th Period - 1:30–3:00

Day B
5th Period - 8:00–9:30
6th Period - 9:35–11:05
Lunch   -   11:10–11:50
7th Period - 11:55–1:25
8th Period - 1:30–3:00

Daily schedule and lesson plans for Mr. King, a junior high school Language Arts teacher:

Mr. King's Language Arts Schedule

1st Period - 8:25 – 9:20 - Literature

2nd Period - 9:25 – 10:20 - English

3rd Period - 10:25 – 11:20 - English

4th Period - 11:25 – 12:20 – Planning Period

Lunch   -   12:25 – 12:55

5th Period -   1:00 – 1:55 - Literature

6th Period -   2:00 – 2:55 - English

7th Period -   3:00 – 3:55 – Journalism

Mr. King's Lesson Plans for Thursday, 6 March:

	LESSON PLANS		
	PERIOD 1 SUBJECT Literature	PERIOD 2 SUBJECT English	PERIOD 3 SUBJECT English
M O N D A Y			
T U E S D A Y			
W E D N E S D A Y			
T H U R S D A Y	American Literature pgs 156-164 Read Beautiful Blue Thinking Critically pg. 165 section 1 #1-4 Answer questions in 1-2 sentences Section 2 #5-8 Pick 2 questions to answer Answers must be written in 8 sentence paragraphs	Review for pronoun test English Grammar pg 185 Review each type of pronoun on pg 205 End of Chapter Review ex 1-5	See period 2
F R I D A Y			

PERIOD 5	PERIOD 6	PERIOD 7
SUBJECT Literature	SUBJECT English	SUBJECT Journalism
See period 1	See period 2	Research Day 8 students to library Remaining students do in-class research

The note Mr. King left for his substitute teacher:

Hello!!

Thank you for teaching my classes today! I don't think you will have any behavior problems. If you do, please make note of the student or students who were disruptive or disrespectful so I can talk to them.

I have two literature classes, three English classes, and a journalism class. The English classes are studying for a test that will be given tomorrow. Please remind them that the test will be TOMORROW! They may work on the End of Chapter Review by dividing into groups of three. Each person is to write down his or her own answers on a sheet of paper. This paper is to go home with the student so he or she can study. Please go over the answers in class. My Teacher's Edition is in the third drawer of my desk.

The literature classes are reading short stories. The story they are to read today is called "Beautiful Blue." The questions they are to answer in the Thinking Critically section will be graded. Therefore they are to work on this assignment by themselves. What they don't finish in class, needs to be done for homework. It is due tomorrow.

The journalism class is working on research papers that are due next Friday. Each student has a famous journalist they are researching. There are eight students that will go to the library to do research there. The list is taped on the blackboard behind my desk. They may go to the library after you have taken attendance. They will stay in the library for the entire period. The remaining students will use the resources in the room to do their research. The list of students that can use the classroom computers today is also taped on the blackboard behind my desk. Each student may use the computer for 20 minutes. Everyone else may use the encyclopedias, newspapers, and magazines in the classroom. The encyclopedias are on the bookshelves. The newspapers and magazines are stacked on top of the table in the back of the room.

If you have any questions, please ask Mrs. Jones in room 215.

Thanks again!

Mr. King

Daily schedule and lesson plans for Mrs. Baker, a high school Spanish teacher:

Mrs. Baker's Daily Schedule

Homeroom – 7:53 – 8:00
1st Period – 8:00 – 8:42 – Spanish 1
2nd Period - 8:45–9:27 – Spanish 4
3rd Period - 9:30–10:12 – Spanish 1
4th Period - 10:15–10:57 – Spanish 1
5th Period - 11:00–11:42 – Lunch
6th Period – 11:45–12:27 – Planning period
7th Period – 12:30–1:12 – Spanish 4
8th Period – 1:15–2:00 – Spanish 4

Mrs. Baker's lesson plans for Wednesday, November 15:

	MONDAY	TUESDAY	WEDNESDAY
PERIOD 1 SPAN 1			Review vocab pg. 35 Workbook pgs 22-24, ex 1-4 Homework- Write 10 sentence paragraph describing your dream house. Use 10 vocab words.
PERIOD 2 SPAN 4			Read pgs 10-15 The Aztecs. Answer questions 1-7, pg 16 Homework- Write 10 sentence paragraph on 3 similarities and 3 differences between the Aztec culture and present day culture of USA.
PERIOD 3 SPAN 1			Follow plan for Period 1
PERIOD 4 SPAN 1			Follow plan for Period 1
PERIOD 7 SPAN 4			Follow plan for Period 2
PERIOD 8 SPAN 4			Follow plan for Period 2

THURSDAY	FRIDAY	NOTES

The note Mrs. Baker left for her substitute teacher:

Dear Substitute Teacher,

Thank you for taking my place today.

Homeroom is from 7:53-8:00. Take attendance using the blue sheet on my desk and hang it outside the door. The students can talk during homeroom, but nothing above a whisper.

<u>Spanish 1</u>

Book and workbook – Buenos Dias.

The objective of the day is to review the "house" vocabulary words and be able to use them to describe a house. I introduced the words on Monday, but I am sure they do not have them memorized yet, so a review is in order. The words are on page 35 of the Buenos Dias book. Please make sure every student turns his or her workbook in to you today when they have completed the work. If they are present today and do not turn in their work, they will not get any credit for it tomorrow. For homework, they are to write a 10-sentence paragraph (in Spanish) describing what their dream home would look like. They are to use at least 10 of the vocabulary words. They can use more if they like.

<u>Spanish 4</u>

Book – The Aztecs

The objective of the day is to learn about the Aztec culture. The stories they are reading are in English so they cannot complain about not understanding the text. Please collect their work whether they have finished or not. For homework, they are to write a 10-sentence (English) paragraph on at least 3 similarities and differences between the Aztec culture and present day culture of the United States. The similarities and differences can come from what they read today and from the video we watched on Tuesday. Please tell them the homework will count for ten points instead of the usual five.

Please tell both classes that their homework will be collected <u>as soon as the bell rings</u> tomorrow.

Lunch is from 11:00-11:42.

My planning period is 5th period from 11:45-12:27.

If you have any questions, please ask Mrs. Daily in Room 210. She can help you with whatever you need.

Thank you,
Mrs. Baker

7

BRINGING THE LESSON PLANS TO LIFE

TIPS, TRICKS, AND IDEAS

Don't worry! The majority of the time, teachers will not have substitute teachers teach anything complicated.

The biggest challenge of working on a lesson is making it interesting. The more interesting a lesson is, the more the students will be involved. The more the students are involved, the more they will learn and the less likely they will be to be distracted or cause problems.

It is important to get to the school early enough so that you will be able to read over the lesson plans, decide how you are going to work on the lesson, and make any necessary preparations. Unless specified in the lesson plans by the teacher, it is up to you how you work on the lesson with the class. Make it fun and use your imagination.

You can have the students work on a lesson by having them complete it:

▶Independently

Students can work on the assignment by themselves at their own pace, must do all of the work themselves and can test their knowledge of a subject and their ability to discover the correct answers.

▶In groups

Students can put their heads together and help each other complete the work. One student may be able to explain a concept to another student who is having problems learning it. By doing this, the student will reinforce what he or she has learned and help a classmate.

▶ As a class

Everyone is involved in the lesson. Students can interact with one another and give different points of view.

Be flexible. Use combinations of the different ways to work on a lesson to keep the students' attention and to keep them interested.

Possible ways to work on the lesson plans left by Mrs. Mills, the second grade teacher:

▶ **Spelling** —"Introduce new spelling words on page 45 of *Spelling Is Fun*. Review words with students. Write words three times each on a sheet of paper to take home and study. Complete and turn in word search worksheet *Spelling is Fun #10.*"

Ways to work on the lesson:

▶ As a class, go over the words. Write the spelling words on the blackboard. Point to each word and have the class repeat it after you. Go over the list again but this time, say the word together once, spell it together, and then repeat the word.

Pick a student to use the word in a sentence to say out loud to the class.

As a small-group activity (2 or 3 students), complete the word search worksheet. The students can help each other find the words.

Independently, when the worksheet is completed, the students will write the words three times each.

▶**Reading**—"Read 'Molly's New Green Coat' on pages 25-35 in *Second Grade Stories*."

Ways to work on the lesson:

▶ As a class, read the story. Pick one student to read a few sentences or one paragraph, depending on the length of the story. When the first student is finished reading, he or she calls on another student to read. That student reads and calls on another until all students have read. When the story is finished, ask a student to give a summary of the story. Ask a few students to tell you their favorite part of the story or to give you reasons why they liked it or did not like it.

▶**Science**—"Watch *Animals of the Desert* video. Answer questions on worksheet and turn in for participation points."

Ways to work on the lesson:

▶ Before students begin watching the video, go over the questions with them so they will know what to pay close attention to in the video. After the video, go over the worksheet with the class. Pick students to answer the questions on the worksheet. If the teacher did not leave an answer key, you may want to watch the video and answer the questions. This prepares you just in case a student has a question or needs an answer. (Note: If a teacher leaves a video for the class to watch but does not leave questions to answer and you feel that the students may need some help paying attention to the video, make up your own questions for them to answer. Have the students write the questions and answers on a sheet of paper and turn it in. You can leave a note explaining to the teacher why you did this.)

▶ **Math**—"Worksheet – Adding Two Columns of Numbers. Students are to complete the worksheet using the small buildings blocks to help them count. Students are to take sheets home and review with parents."

Ways to work on the lesson:

▶ Have the students complete the worksheet independently. To check their work, when all students are finished, have a few students at a time go to the chalkboard.

Give each student a different problem to write and answer on the chalkboard. Go over the answers with the class. Repeat until all the problems have been solved.

Ideas for how to work on Mr. King's language arts assignments:

▶**Literature—**"American Literature pgs. 156-164. Read "Beautiful Blue."

Thinking Critically pg 165. Section One - #1–4. Answer questions in 1–2 sentences. Section Two - #5–8. Pick two questions to answer in 8-sentence paragraphs."

Ways to work on the lesson:

▶Have the students take turns reading the story. Call on one student to begin reading when that student has finished, have them pick another student to continue the story. When they have completed the story, have them work on the questions independently.

Or have the students read the story silently to themselves. When they are finished, call on students to give summaries of the story and discuss it with them. Have the students work on the assignment when you are finished discussing.

▶**English—**"Review for Pronoun test. *English Grammar* pg. 185, review each type of pronoun. Page 205 - *End of Chapter Review,* ex. 1-5."

Ways to work on the lesson:

▶Review pronouns with the class by picking a student to explain and/or write on the chalkboard each type of pronoun. Allow students to divide into groups of three after the review is complete. Walk around and help each group as needed. Go over answers in class when all of the groups have completed the work.

Or you can turn the review day into a game by dividing the class into two groups. Give them a few minutes to review the types of pronouns and the End of Chapter Review. When you are ready to begin, have the students close and put away their books. Call on students from each group to answer review questions, alternate between the groups and go up and down each row of students so that you make sure everyone has a turn. Give one point for questions answered correctly. Record the correct answers to the End of Chapter Review on the chalkboard or an overhead projector. When all of the questions have been answered, the group with the most points wins. Have students write down the answers on a sheet of paper to take home and review.

▶ **Journalism—**"Research day. Eight students to library. Remaining students – do in-class research."

Ways to work on the lesson:

▶ Allow the students doing research in the library to go. Give computer time to the students who are signed up for it. The remaining students are to complete their research independently. Help them locate information as needed.

Ideas for how to work on Mrs. Baker's Spanish lessons:

▶ **Spanish 1**—"Review vocabulary page 35. Workbook pgs. 22-24, ex 1-4.

<u>Homework</u> - Write a 10-sentence paragraph describing your dream house, use at least 10 new vocabulary words."

Ways to work on the lesson:

▶ As a class, review the vocabulary. You can say the word in English and pick students to answer in Spanish or vice versa. You can also pick students to go to the front of the room to "be the teacher" and call on other students to translate the words.

Have the students complete exercises 1-4 in groups and turn in their workbooks when finished.

Another way to review the words is to turn the vocabulary review into a game. Divide the class into two groups. Give a word to one student from each group. The first one to answer scores a point for their team. The team with the most points wins.

Have the students complete the workbook exercises independently when the review game is over and turn it in when complete.

Homework- If there is still time left in the period, have the students start working on their homework independently.

▶**Spanish 4**—"Read pages 10-15, *The Aztecs.* Answer questions 1-7, pg 16.

Homework- Write a 10-sentence paragraph on at least three similarities and differences between the Aztec culture and the culture of the United States."

Ways to work on the lesson:

▶As a class, read pages 10-15. Have every student read a few sentences or a paragraph of the story, depending on the length.

In groups of two or three, have the students answer questions 1-7.

Or have the students work silently, reading and answering the questions by themselves.

Homework. If there is still time left in the period, have the students start working on their homework independently.

Some things to remember when the students are working on an assignment:

▶ The pace of a lesson is very important. If the lesson is moving too slowly, the students will get bored and lose interest. If the lesson is moving too quickly, the students will not understand the material being taught, get frustrated, and lose interest. Watch the way the students react to what you are teaching. If they start to get distracted and talk a lot, it may be a sign that the pace is too slow. If they start to ask a lot of questions and seem frustrated, it could be that the lesson is too fast. You must find a happy medium that is slow enough so the students understand and fast enough so that they don't get bored.

▶ Junior high and high school teachers often teach the same lesson during different periods of the day. For each period, you can evaluate how you presented the lesson. If the way you worked on the lesson did not work or the students were not as involved as you hoped, you can change your presentation for the next period. If the group activity during first period science class was a disaster, make it an individual assignment for the next class. Try different approaches to the lesson to keep the students involved and interested. If everything is going great, keep doing what is working.

►Remember and remind the students that group work only works as long as they are working quietly together on the assignment. If the noise level is too high or they are not working on the assignment, break the groups up and have students do the work by themselves.

►When you give a class an assignment that is to be completed independently or in groups, walk around the room to check on their progress. Walking around the classroom lets students know that you are interested in how and what they are doing. It allows you to make sure they are on task, check their progress, and possibly help someone who is afraid to raise his or her hand to get help.

►Be patient with the students. Some students may not work as fast as the others or may not catch on as quickly. Take your time with these students and realize that they are trying to do the work. For any student who seems to be struggling, take a few minutes to help him or her understand the lesson. Get the rest of the class started on the assignment, then go back to the student and explain anything that he or she does not understand.

▶ As you are walking through the aisles, beware the backpacks!! They like to wrap themselves around your ankles and pull you to the floor where they can get a better look at you. Laughter will erupt louder than you can possibly imagine, and any pain you feel will quickly flush your face exposing your embarrassment.

If the students do have their backpacks on the floor, ask them to put them totally under their desks and step very, very carefully through the aisles.

▶ You may find yourself in the situation where your students either do not want to do, complain about, or have already done the work the teacher has set out for them. This can be a hard situation because you want the students to do their work and they may refuse. Explain that it is what the teacher left as an assignment, maybe for extra help with the topic or as a review. Remind them that if they have done it before, then they should be able to complete it quickly because they already know the answers.

You may have to negotiate with your students to get them to do the work. Offer them options for which you both like the end result. They get something fun to do and they complete their work. Tell them that once everyone has finished the work, they will be able to play a game. Or, offer them the chance to talk quietly once the work is finished.

▶ If the lesson the teacher left for you is not working and the students have no clue what you are trying to explain, consider taking a break from it for a few minutes. Play a quick game or tell the students to stand up and stretch, then try going back to the lesson. If it still isn't working, do something else. Review a previous lesson with the students or give them a subject-specific worksheet or word search to complete. It is better to work on something you understand and can explain than to totally confuse the students.

If by chance a teacher doesn't anticipate being absent and does not leave a lesson plan don't panic! Use your creativity and your Just-In-Case Bag to get you through the day.

▶ Pass out your learning activity worksheets, subject specific worksheets, crossword puzzles and /or coloring pages from your Just-In-Case Bag. Read the storybook you brought in or watch the movie you brought.

▶ Ask another teacher in the same grade level or subject whether he or she knows what the absent teacher is working on with the class. If you are able to get a general idea of what the class is working on, you can improvise a lesson. For example, if a class is studying multiplication, make up a few multiplication problems and write them on the chalkboard or on an overhead projector transparency. Have the students copy them down on a sheet of paper and answer them. When all students have completed the work, call on different students to give you the answers.

▶ If they are reading a story about bravery, have them write a short paragraph about someone who did something brave or about what bravery means to them.

▶ If they are learning new spelling words, have them write a story using the new words. Another option is to create a story as a class. Write a sentence on the overhead projector. Call on students to add a sentence to the story that uses one of the spelling words. Add onto the story until all of the spelling words have been used or each student has had a turn.

▶ If the class is studying Geography, you can give them a list of longitude and latitude coordinates and have them find the points on the map.

▶ Read the class a story, but do not read the ending. Have the students draw a picture or write a paragraph to express how they predict the story will end. Go over what the students draw or write and have them explain why they believe the story will end that way. Read the end of the story to them. Compare their endings with the book ending.

▶ If it is close to a holiday, the students can use construction paper and markers or crayons to make greeting cards for their parents, friends, or teacher.

▶ Use the Internet. A terrific resource for quick and easy lesson plans is the Internet. Type the words "lesson plans" into any search engine and it will pull up several websites with usable lesson plans. Many of the Web sites allow you to choose lesson plans by grade level, subject, and topic. On some sites, when you click on the lesson plan you want, it will pull up the author of the lesson plan, the title of the activity or lesson, an overview or purpose of the lesson, materials needed, a description, and suggestions for using it in class. Other sites may have worksheets that can be printed and used in class.

▶ An option for junior high and high school students is to give them time to study or complete homework from another class. This works only if they are quiet and working on homework and not sleeping.

8

WELCOME TO CLASS

The first time you see the students in your class, your stomach may flip-flop or your palms may sweat. Remember to relax. They may be surprised to see a substitute instead of their regular teacher. They don't know you and they don't know what to expect from you.

This is your opportunity to start the day off positively:

▶ Introduce yourself and get to know students' names. Let them know what you expect from them and what they can expect from you.

▶ Greet the students with a smile and *"Hello"* or *"Good Morning"* as they enter the classroom. Shortly before the bell rings, start directing them to sit in their seats. Immediately after the bell rings, make sure all students are in their assigned seats and quiet before you start talking.

▶ Inform the students that their teacher will not be in class and that you will be there in his or her place for the day.

▶ Write your name on the chalkboard to help them remember it.

▶ Take attendance. As you go through the attendance list, try and put faces and names together. Learning the students' names quickly will be valuable to you during the day or class. It is better to call a student by his name instead of "little boy in the blue shirt."

Most teachers have a seating chart. A seating chart may be squares drawn on a piece of paper to represent the desks in the classroom. Inside each square is the name of the student who sits at that desk. Using the seating chart allows you to easily and quickly identify a student by his or her name. If there isn't a seating chart, it may be worthwhile to make one of your own.

One way to definitely know the names of the students is to have them make name cards to put on their desks or give them an index card to write their name on and tape to the corner of their desk. (To make a name card, have the students fold a half sheet of paper, so that it will stand on their desks like a tent. Have the students write their names on the cards and face them toward the front of the room.)

► Go over the rules and consequences quickly with the students. Most teachers have a copy of their rules and consequences posted on the chalkboard, bulletin board, or in their sub folder. Explain to the class that even though their regular teacher is not there, the rules and consequences still apply. This lets the students know that you intend to follow and enforce the rules and consequences.

▶ If you plan to use an attention getting signal (Chapter 3), explain it to them, why you will use it, and what they need to do if you give it. Practice it a few times, so they will recognize it and know what to do when you give it.

▶ Explain the assignment they will be doing and begin working on it.

Here is an example of what you might say:

"Good morning everyone. Thank you for taking your seats and being quiet. My name is Ms. Simmons. I will be here today for your teacher, Mr. Liggins. Let's see who is here and who is absent today. (Take attendance.) Now, let's quickly go over the rules so I learn them and you get a refresher of what is expected. (Go over the classroom rules and consequences.) I also want to show you a signal that I will use if I need to get everyone's attention. When I use this signal it means that you are to stop what you are doing, stop talking, stop moving, and look at me. (Practice the attention getting signal.) Ok, let's start working on today's lesson."

9

GAINING AND KEEPING CONTROL IN THE CLASSROOM

It is important to establish control of the classroom from the second the students enter the room. Being in control of a classroom means that the students complete assignments, listen and follow your instructions promptly, are seated and working quietly, respond when you talk to the class in a normal volume speaking voice, and are paying attention. If a problem occurs, it can be handled in a calm manner without it being too much of a disruption. The students feel comfortable in class and, in turn, you feel comfortable being there.

Rarely do students enter the classroom quietly, immediately sit in their assigned seats, and patiently wait for you to begin class. As soon as the students come in to the classroom, take time to get them settled down, in their seats, quiet, and looking at and listening to you.

If they are not settling down quickly enough by themselves, help them along by saying things like:

▶ *"Please sit in your assigned seats. It's time for class to begin."*

▶ *"Quiet down, please."*

▶ *"Please stop talking. We are ready to begin."*

▶ *"It's time to begin. Please take your seats and focus your attention on me."*

▶ *"Please show me that you can do what I am asking you to do."*

When you are speaking to the class:

▶ Make sure all of the students are quiet and paying attention to you. If you try to talk over a few students, you will quickly lose the whole class. If you try to talk over the whole class, you will not get anything done.

▶ Use a strong, firm tone of voice to speak to the students. They will understand that you mean what you say. The more octaves you raise your voice, the more you will sound like you are unsure of what you are telling them. If you yell and scream, you will sound like you don't know what you are doing or don't know how to handle a class of students.

▶ Correct unacceptable behavior immediately. As soon as a student breaks a rule or is being disruptive, let the student know that he or she has done something against the rules or is disrupting the other students and needs to stop immediately. The longer you allow a student to exhibit the behavior, the longer it will take to get the student to behave in an acceptable manner and the longer it will disrupt the class.

▶ Enforce the rules and consequences of the class. All of the rules apply to all of the students all of the time. It is not fair to let one student break a rule and to punish the next student for doing the same thing. Be consistent!

▶ Use your body language. Body language shows how you are feeling without one word coming out of your mouth. Looking at a student and shaking your head or your finger "no" is sometimes enough for the student to know that he or she needs to stop and get back on task.

If you use a stern face, the students will understand that you are serious. If you smile, they will understand that you are being nice or approving.

Be careful not to mix facial expressions and tones of voice. The students will be confused about what you mean. If you are serious, use a serious face and a firm tone of voice. If you are praising someone for a job well done, smile and use a cheery tone of voice. Do not smile while correcting a student's inappropriate behavior. The student will not know whether you are being serious or joking.

▶ Be visible. When you are talking or giving instruction, stand in front of the class. This makes you visible to the students and shows them that you are taking an active role in the class and are interested their learning. The more you sit behind the teacher's desk, the less visible you are to the students and the more likely they are to cause problems. Get up and walk around. Check their work. Make sure they are free from objects that will distract them. The more they see you, the more they know you are there to help them and to keep them in line.

Your day will run more smoothly once the students understand that you will not tolerate misbehaving. You will feel more confident and be able to concentrate on teaching the students if you are on top of the game.

10

ENFORCING THE CLASSROOM RULES AND CONSEQUENCES

It would be an ideal teaching environment if every student in every class behaved according to all of the rules all of the time. Half of the challenges of being a teacher would disappear. Unfortunately, sooner or later you will run into a student who causes disruptions or misbehaves. Schools and teachers establish rules to maintain order and consequences to discipline students who break rules.

It is very important that you enforce the rules and consequences. By enforcing them, you will keep control of the classroom. When students know that you will discipline them for inappropriate behavior, they will be less likely to misbehave and you will be able to maintain a good classroom environment.

The best way to handle behavior problems in the classroom is to educate yourself. Learn the rules and consequences, what disciplinary actions the school uses, what actions you can and cannot take, and the names of the principal, vice-principal, and any other staff who deal with discipline issues.

A teacher will establish classroom rules and consequences according to what is most important to him or her and how he or she wants the classroom to run. For some teachers, behaving properly in class may be more important than having the students always complete assignments.

Most teachers have a list of their rules and consequences posted in a place in the classroom where the students can see them every day. This gives the students a visual reminder of what is expected of them and what they can expect when they don't follow the rules. When you are in a classroom where the rules and consequences are posted, follow those rules. The students are familiar with them and know what to expect for a consequence if they break a rule. Teachers may also explain any special systems they have for discipline in the note they leave for you.

If a teacher does not have lists posted, it is a good idea to have your own set of rules and consequences that are important for you. Tell the class your rules verbally or write them on a piece of poster board and put them in a place visible to all students. Go over them at the beginning of the class so the students know that they will have to behave accordingly.

Examples of classroom rules are:
▶ Stay in your seat unless given permission to get up.
▶ Keep your hands and feet to yourself.
▶ Do not touch other students' property.
▶ Raise your hand and wait to be called on before speaking.
▶ No food, drinks, or candy are to be eaten during class.
▶ Be on time to class.
▶ Respect yourself and your classmates.
▶ Respect everyone's right to learn.
▶ Listen when others speak.

Consequences are set to discipline students who do not follow the rules. Teachers create consequences according to the school rules and/ or their own system of disciplining bad behavior.

Most teachers have their own system for handling problems in the classroom and giving consequences. They usually start off with a small correction like a verbal warning. If the disruptive behavior continues, the consequences become increasingly tougher.

Examples of consequences are:
- ▶ **Using nonverbal gestures.** Shake your head or forefinger "no."
- ▶ **Verbal warning.** Tell the student what rule he or she is breaking or how he or she is disrupting the class. Let the student know that he or she is being warned.
- ▶ **Name on the board.** Write the name of the student on the board. At the end of the day, include students' names in the note you leave for the teacher, and explain the students' behavior.
- ▶ **Move to a different seat.** Move the student to a desk away from other students.
- ▶ **Sit out for five minutes of recess.** Take away five minutes of recess. Increase the amount of time they lose in small increments if the behavior continues. (Usually used with elementary school students and middle school students if they have recess.)
- ▶ **After-school detention.** Write a student up for after school detention. (Usually

used with middle school and high school students.)

▶ **Give the student an official "write-up."** The student may have to meet with a counselor to talk about the write-up and his or her behavior. (Usually used with middle and high school students.)

▶ **Remove the student from the classroom.** Talk to another teacher in the same grade level or subject to find out whether that teacher is willing to take a student who is being disruptive into his or her classroom. Send a student to that teacher when the student is behaving in a way that you cannot handle (repeatedly disrupting, constantly trying to argue with you, not doing the assignment and bothering other students) while keeping control of the other students.

▶ **Send the student to the principal's office.** This should be used only in situations when the student is being extremely disruptive, disrespectful to you or another student, or physically hurting another student.

When disciplining a student, be sure to follow the consequence system and make sure the punishment fits the rule broken. For example, if a student gets out of his or her seat without permission, give the student a verbal warning and remind him or her stay seated unless given permission to get up. It would be a bit extreme to send this student to the principal's office for this offense.

When disciplining a student, do it in a way that gets your point across to the student, but do not humiliate the student in front of the class.
- ▶ Pull the student aside and talk to him or her in a low voice.
- ▶ Tell the student they are exhibiting behavior that is inappropriate.
- ▶ Tell the student what you would like him or her to do
- ▶ Inform the student what consequence you are giving him or her for the inappropriate behavior.

When a student has misbehaved, let the teacher know what happened and how you handled it. The teacher may want to address the problem with the student. It may be a long-term problem the student is working on improving, and your input to the teacher may help with the process.

It is very important that you enforce the rules of the classroom and follow through with any promised consequences.

Some ideas on how to handle a student who is:

▶ **Not paying attention.** Call the students' name and ask whether he or she agrees with what you said, or ask them for a summary of what is going on.

▶ **Talking.** Try telling the student, *"I know what you have to say is important, but I need you to stop talking and follow along with the rest of us"* or *"I know what you have to say is important, but please wait until you are out of the classroom so your friend can give you all the attention you deserve."*

▶ **Getting out of his or her seat.** Politely tell the student to sit down. Volunteer this student to be the first one to give an answer to a problem.

▶ **Throwing things.** Explain that throwing items in the classroom could hurt another student. Have the student pick the item up and put it back where it belongs. If it is trash, have the student throw it away and pick up a few pieces of trash around his or her desk.

► **Fighting.** Send the student to the principal's office or call school security into the classroom.

► **Not doing the work.** Work with the student on a few problems. Tell him or her to keep going and that you will be back to help after you check on other students.

► **Arguing.** If the students are sitting close to each other, separate them. If the arguing continues, get the rest of the class going on their assignment. Privately, talk to the students with the problem and try to come to a resolution. You may not be able to reach a solution with them, but maybe they will understand that arguing and causing a distraction in class in not appropriate.

► **Bad language.** Say, *"I do not appreciate that type of language. Do not use it in this classroom."*

► **Distracted by a cellular phone, Discman or other toys.** Most schools do not allow cellular phones or other electronic devices be used by the students during the school day. Say *"Please put that away and join the rest of us so you don't fall behind."* If the student continues to play with the item, have him or her put it on your desk until the end of the day or class period.

Phrases to help curb bad behavior:

▶ *"I would appreciate it if you would..."*

▶ *"It would make me so happy if you..."*

▶ *"A good choice for you to make right now would be..."*

11

GOOD-TO-KNOW INFO TO GET YOU THROUGH THE DAY

During the day, there may be a variety of events that take place in and out of the classroom.

Here are some examples:

▶**Assemblies**

Assemblies are a fun break from the normal school day. Many assemblies are interactive and will have the students clapping their hands, stomping their feet, dancing, and singing. There may be students who are not interested in what is going on. Keep these students from bothering others who are enjoying the assembly. You will either have to sit with or stand beside your class to keep students behaving properly, and paying attention to the speakers, dancers, or singers. Move any student who is causing problems closer to you. Take a sheet of paper to write down the names of misbehaving students. Include their names and how they were disruptive in the note you leave for the teacher.

▶ Be Prepared for Unexpected Changes

You may accept an assignment for the Chemistry teacher, but when you get to the school they tell you they need you to substitute for the Physical Education teacher instead. Instances like this are rare, but they do happen. Keep an open mind. Be flexible. This situation may be to your benefit. You may discover that the new assignment is one you enjoy and accept every time it is available.

Be prepared. In the trunk of your car, keep a spare set of clothes and shoes that you can wear in the gym, in case you were expecting to have a classroom assignment and they need you to substitute for the physical education teacher instead.

If you do not want to accept the change, the school may be able to find another assignment in the subject area you want at another school. If they cannot, be prepared not to work that day.

►**Homeroom**

Homeroom is a period during the day when middle and high school students go to their assigned classroom and receive important information, handouts, fill out paperwork, have attendance taken, or any other tasks. Homeroom may be the first period of the day, around lunch time, or the last period of the day. Even though you do not teach during homeroom, the students still have to behave according to the rules.

►**Lunch**

Whether you bring your lunch or buy it from the cafeteria, I suggest you get out of the classroom and go to the teachers' lounge, another classroom, or your car to eat. Even if it is only for twenty minutes, it is a refresher to get out of the room you are teaching in and get a quick change of scenery. It is a great stress reliever to talk to other teachers, laugh, vent your frustrations, or read a good book or magazine.

►**Passes**

Passes give students permission to be in the hallways to go to the restroom, the library, the clinic, the computer lab, or any number of places in the school when normally they should be in class. In the beginning of the day, find out the school's policy on giving out passes. It may be your decision to allow students to go to the restroom during class.

If students complete an assignment early and have free time before the end of class, they may ask to go to another room, for example the library or the gym. The librarian or physical education teacher may have specific times for these visits or they may limit the number of students allowed to enter. Check to see what the policy is on sending students to other classrooms or areas before you let them go. Do not send students to other classrooms without knowing whether they are allowed to go or without permission from the teacher.

A good way to keep tabs on who is out of the room is to have students write their names on a sheet of paper with the time they leave the room and the time they come back. This record will help you if you have to tell a teacher about a student who spent twenty minutes getting a drink at the water fountain right outside the door or a student who went to the restroom at the beginning of class and didn't come back until two minutes before the end of class.

▶ **Planning Period**

Teachers are given time during the day to prepare lesson plans, grade papers, or complete school-related work. For substitutes, the teacher's planning period is time to prepare yourself for the next group of students or the next activity, put collected papers in order, read over the lesson plan, start writing a note to the teacher, or review the next lesson you will teach.

When you are prepped for the next activity or group of students, take a few minutes to refresh yourself. Relax! Take a break! Read a book! Do whatever it takes for you to refresh yourself and get ready to continue.

There may be times when you have to cover for another class during your teacher's planning period. The main office will inform you if you will be needed to substitute in another classroom and give you all the information needed for that class.

▶ Praise

Praising students for a job well done, good listening skills, or any other positive action they have done is very important. Students like to feel that their hard work is being appreciated and that it is worth it to continue behaving properly or doing a good job on their work.

Praise students whenever they answer a question correctly, do something nice for their classmate, play nicely or are following the rules.

▶ Praise phrases:

Good Job!

Nice work!

Way to go!

I knew you could do it!

I like the way you are all quietly working on your assignment!

You all are showing me how well behaved you can be; that is great!

You got it!

You are so smart!

A little bit of encouragement from you is felt many times over by students. Letting them know that you appreciate their hard work or good behavior makes it more likely that they will behave as well in the future.

▶ **Questions**

Do not be afraid to ask questions. Most teachers will happily answer any questions you have and are willing to help you in any way they can. If something does not make sense to you, ask another teacher to explain it. It is important to understand what you are to do, feel confident doing it, and avoid confusion.

▶ **Recess**

Most elementary and middle school students get two recess periods, one in the morning and one after lunch. Recess can be indoors or outdoors, weather permitting. Outdoor recess is a time when students can run around, scream, play to their hearts' content, and, most importantly, burn off some of their excess energy. Indoor recess is a time when students can play a game by themselves or with a friend, play with the toys in the classroom, talk, or read. Your class may have specific recess times. If there are no specific recess times, it may be up to you as to when you give them play time. If you go outside, be sure to have a bell or whistle to signal the students when it is time to line up to go inside. If you have recess inside, set a timer to let them know when it is time to clean up and start working again.

High school students normally don't get a recess period. Some schools may give the students a long break (between 10-15 minutes) during the day, but they normally are not allowed to leave the building.

► **School Announcements**

School announcements usually occur shortly after school begins in the morning and in the afternoon just before school ends. They contain useful information for the students, from the lunch menu to after-school events. Pay attention and make sure the students are quiet so they hear what is going on for that day. There may be important information such as an assembly or a change in the daily schedule that the main office forgot to tell you.

▶ **Show Respect to Get Respect**

You want to create a good atmosphere in the classroom. You want to be able to speak to your students and have them speak to you with respect. If you yell and scream at the students, they will probably try and yell and scream at you.

When you show respect, courtesy, politeness, and thoughtfulness toward the students, they are more likely to show these same kinds of sentiments toward you. When you are respectful towards the students, accept only the same politeness and courtesy back from them. Talk to them in the same manner as you want them to talk to you. *"Raymond, I did not yell when I was talking to you, and I do not like it that you are yelling at me. Please lower your voice when you are talking to me."*

When taking assignments for high school, I quickly learned that a lot of the kids want to be treated as though they were adults. I started calling the boys "Sir" and the girls "Ma'am." This is surprisingly effective. When you give them a title, they feel obligated to respond in an adult-like manner. Most returned the courtesy by calling me "Ma'am."

Don't forget to add "please" and "thank you" to any request you have or to show your appreciation. Remind the students to use "please" and "thank you" when speaking to you and to others.

How you treat your students is how you can expect them to treat you. Take the time to tell and show them respectful ways. Give and accept only the best behavior.

▶ **Special Classes**

Special classes may include Physical Education, Art, or Music. The students may go to another classroom for these classes or the teacher may come into your classroom to teach. If the students go to another classroom, it is important to get them to the special class on time and to pick them up on time. The teachers appreciate it. They have only a limited amount of time for each class, and every second counts.

▶ **Special-Needs Students**

Be aware that it is possible to have students in your class who have special needs. A special-needs student may learn more slowly or in a different way than the others, be hyperactive, have a hearing, sight, or speech impairment, or have a physical handicap. A special-needs student may require more of your time and attention than the other students in the classroom. It can be challenging to work with this student and keep the rest of the classroom going.

If the student is hyperactive, make him or her the helper for the day. Give him or her extra tasks to keep busy, like passing out the crayons or collecting the papers. The more he or she has to do, the less time he or she has to be distracted or become a distraction to the other students.

If the student learns more slowly than the rest of the class, you may need to spend extra time with this student to help him or her understand the assignment. Be patient. Realize that he or she is trying.

If a student has a physical handicap, he or she may have a specially designed seat, may need help moving from class to class, or may need to leave class early.

Please, take care not to embarrass a student with a special need. He or she may already be sensitive about the disability and if you point it out in front of the class, this may further embarrass him or her.

▶ **Student Helpers**

Student helpers are students who are repeatedly picked by the teacher to do various tasks because they are reliable, loyal, intelligent; work hard to complete all assignments; receive good grades; will inform you if fellow classmates misbehave; pay attention all of the time, and know exactly how everything is run.

Many times a teacher will let you know the names of students who are good helpers. If you have any questions or need something done, ask this student.

▶ **Take Something to Read**

There may be times when you find yourself staring at the walls waiting for the students to complete an assignment or for time to pass by until the next class begins. You have walked through the aisles three times, asked all the students twice if they need any help and now, on your third walk through, the students are beginning to feel watched instead of helped. Teachers have other work they can do while waiting, like grading papers or making lesson plans for the next week, but substitute teachers may find themselves with time on their hands. During these times, a book, magazine, or newspaper can be your salvation from substitute teacher boredom. Be sure to periodically check on the students to ensure that they are still on task.

12

DON'T BECOME A SUBSTITUTE GONE CRAZY

For Goodness Sake, DON'T CRY!!

I've heard stories about substitute teachers who ran out of the classroom because the students teased them to the point of tears. One story I remember hearing involved a brand new substitute teacher and three students. One student started to tease the substitute about her accent. Another teased her about her hair, and a third decided to talk about her shoes. Instead of ignoring them, she started to take offense. The more upset she got the deeper the students dug. In less than fifteen minutes, the students had succeeded in breaking her spirit and making her cry. Don't let this happen to you!!

Some students will try to push substitute teachers to their limit and be disrespectful because it's fun for them. It is a game to see how far they can go and how upset they can make a substitute teacher. When a substitute teacher runs out of the classroom crying, the students have succeeded in their game. The substitute teacher that does cry has probably lost all of the possible respect he or she could get out of the students and will probably be powerless if he or she decides to substitute again in that school.

As a substitute teacher, you have to have thick skin. You cannot take personally anything that the students say about you. Kids can be cruel, intentionally or unintentionally.

If you are a bit overweight, they may tease you about it. If you have big eyes, a big nose, or a big mouth, watch out. Those body parts are fair game for teasing. If they say, "You are so fat it looks like you ate a whale for breakfast," respond by saying, "No, actually I ate two" or "No, I only eat whale on the weekends. Today I had a cow."

Respond in a way that shows students that their silly taunts have no effect on you. The moment you start taking offense at what they are saying, they will have the upper hand. Ignore what they say. Laugh at it. You have to be confident in yourself. Show them that your self-confidence is stronger than anything they throw at you. And, honestly, do you care what they think of you?

Remember, "Sticks and stones will break my bones, but words will never hurt me." When you don't allow their teasing to have an effect on you, they will quickly get bored and drop it because you aren't responding the way they hoped. They don't have anything to feed off of and the fun is taken out of their game.

Of course, there may be a student who crosses the line from teasing to insulting. He or she may make a racial, sexual, or religious comment that has no place in the classroom. Firmly tell the student that the comment was inappropriate and to watch what he or she says. If you feel it is something that needs to be further looked into, inform their teacher and/or the principal.

Don't Blow Up!

It is tough to keep your cool if there is a student who is yelling and screaming in your face or who hasn't listened to a word you have said all day. Don't let either of these bad behaviors make you so angry that you blow up.

The instant you engage yourself in a screaming match with a student, you have lost control of yourself. You have allowed yourself to become angry at someone who has a problem and only knows how to show it by exhibiting inappropriate behavior. The misbehaving student may be intentionally trying get you upset for one reason or another. Don't let this child succeed in his quest for an argument.

You have to be in control of yourself and keep your emotions under control. Before you begin to speak to this student, take a deep breath and hold it for ten seconds. In those ten seconds, try to release all of your anger. Put what you are going to say in the shortest, most direct sentence possible. Speak in a quiet but firm voice. The louder the student gets, the quieter you should get. It may be hard, but remain calm. Always think that you can handle any situation with a calm and collected attitude and you will come out on top.

If the student sees that his or her tactics are not working on you and decides to sit down and return to the land of the normal, allow him or her to do so. If the student cannot regain control, send him or her to another teacher's classroom to cool down for a while.

Never Hurt a Student!

NEVER hit a student! NEVER do back to a student what he or she did to you! If a student bites you, do not under any circumstances bite the student back. If you do, you will find yourself in a world of trouble. You may face jail time, the parents may sue you, and you can forget about ever substitute teaching again.

If a student attempts to hit you, try to get out the way before he makes contact with you. If a student does bite or hit you, call the office immediately! Explain what happened and have the student removed from the class.

Students know that they should not physically hurt others, especially teachers. A student should have no reason to lay a hand on you, and you should have no reason to hit a student either.

Do not humiliate a student by insulting his or her clothing, appearance, intelligence level, social status, or financial level as a way to shame him or her into good behavior. Most students have to deal with their peers teasing them; they should not have to worry about a teacher hurting their feelings too. Any unkind words that you say to a student are a bad choice on your part.

13
LAUGH IT UP

When a student tells a funny, clean, joke or story, or does something funny that is not harmful or hurtful to another student or you, laugh at it. It will make you feel good to be able to share a laugh with your students.

Students have shared their jokes and stories with me. It made me feel closer to them. It lets the students know that you are human and you do have a sense of humor.

Kindergarten

It was the first day of school and I had an assignment for a week as a kindergarten teacher's assistant. As the first day of school often goes, there was a bit of confusion on the students' part as to what to do. The teacher and I were passing out papers when one little girl began to howl. I went over to her desk, bent down, and asked her "Nina, what are you doing?"

"I'm a werewolf," she replied, "and werewolves make this sound, OOOOOOOOOOOOOOOOOO."

I said, "Well, that is great, but don't you know that werewolves aren't allowed in school?"

She looked at me and smiled. Then she reached over, pinched my cheek, and said, "OK, cutie."

High School Spanish Class

The class joke teller decided he had a great joke that would make everyone think and laugh.

"OK, I got one for you," he announced to me and the class. "Say 'shop' five times."

A brave classmate decided to play along. "Shop, shop, shop, shop, shop."

"What do you do at a green light?"

"Stop."

"Really? Most people GO at a green light"

"Oh yeah, that's what I meant. Only people who don't know how to drive stop at green lights. I was talking about what you do at a red light…"

His explanation went on for about another minute as the entire class roared with laughter.

High School English Class

When I was substitute teaching for a high school English teacher, I was the recipient of a prank. The students were taking turns reading a story from their textbook out loud when the classroom phone rang. I asked the student who was reading to stop for a minute and I answered the phone. "Mr. Carlton's room." Silence on the other end. I repeated myself a bit louder. "Mr. Carlton's room." Still no answer. I held on for a few more seconds, and then hung up.

The student began reading again. A few minutes later the phone rang again. I answered, but still the other end was silent. I began to wonder whether there was a problem with the phone line and figured if there were an emergency someone from the office would come and tell us about it.

We started reading the story again and for a third time, the phone rang. At this point I was feeling a bit frustrated. Things in the class were going along great and the students seemed to be interested in the story. I didn't want any distractions to break the flow of the class. I walked toward the phone, picked up the receiver, and raised it to my ear. Before I could say anything, I could hear a grumble on the other end. Fearing that someone was in trouble, I asked, "Are you OK?" The grumble quickly erupted into a wild laughter that I could hear on the phone and in the classroom. The laughter quickly spread to the other students. I looked up to see a student holding a cellular phone bent over with laughter. He had been the one calling the classroom phone and thought it was hilarious to prank the substitute teacher. I imagine it was a funny scene to see the substitute teacher run from one end of the classroom to the other to answer a prank phone call. The giggles infected me and I laughed with the class.

14

A NOTE FOR YOU, A NOTE FOR ME

After the bell rings and the students have left or you have taken them to their dismissal point, get ready to go home. Neatly organize the books, papers, and other materials you used so the teacher can find them. Label the work you collected from the students (Math worksheets, Science worksheets, assignments-1st period). Clear the teacher's desk of your belongings and trash.

Write a note about how it went. Teachers like to know what happened while they were gone so they know where to pick up, can praise a job well done, or address any problems.

Let the teacher know how your day went by writing a brief note. The note you leave for the teacher is important because it is your account of what went on for that day.

Topics to include in your note:

▶ Your name

▶ How you worked on the lessons

▶ What the class finished or did not have enough time to complete

▶ What you did not understand in the lesson plans

▶ Where you put any collected work

▶ Who was helpful

▶ How hard the class worked to complete their assignments

▶ Whether you encountered any behavior problems

▶ How you handled any problems

▶ Any other incidents that happened during the day that you believe the teacher needs to know about

Here is an example of a note left to Mr. Malone a High School Science teacher:

Mr. Malone,

My name is Melanie Evans. I was your substitute teacher on Tuesday the 10th. I just wanted to leave you a few notes on how the day went.

Biology—Periods 1, 3, 5

To complete the assignment, I divided the class into five groups. Each group worked on a section of the assignment. When the groups were finished, each stood up and presented their answers to the class. Each student had to present part of the answer. Each group turned in the work they did on their section.

This worked pretty well. The students did a good job on their presentations and seemed to enjoy giving their answers to the class.

Advanced Biology—Periods 2, 6

The students handed in their homework from yesterday. They took turns reading pages 95-98 out loud. They answered the questions in the *Testing Your Knowledge* section independently.

All of the work I collected is in your blue folder on top of your desk.

I did not have any behavior problems today. The students were great!

Thank you,

Melanie Evans

When you have finished the note for the teacher, write one for yourself.

Include:

- ►Ways you presented the lesson
- ►How it worked for you
- ►Things you might try next time
- ►Things that didn't work
- ►Your thoughts about the class
- ►Whether the students were well behaved
- ►Who in the class needs a little more attention or help than the other students
- ►How you handled problems in the class
- ►Your thoughts about the teacher:
    - ►How organized the teacher was
    - ►Whether he or she left clear lesson plans
    - ►Whether the materials were easy to find
    - ►Whether you would substitute teach for that teacher again

The teacher will appreciate the note you write for him or her. Leave the note for your teacher on top of his or her desk so it is the first thing the teacher will see. Keep all of the notes you write for yourself in a notebook. Whenever you need to remember how a day went with one particular class or review how you taught a lesson, you will have your notes for reference.

When all is done, you are ready to leave. Go to the main office and sign out. Take a deep breath and pat yourself on the back! You did it!! Good job!!!

15

LET IT GO

I wish that every day you substitute will be an easy, fulfilling day in which you are able to help the students with their assignments and the students are well behaved and respectful. Unfortunately, there will be days that test your patience, days when nothing goes right, days when the kids will almost drive you up the wall. Don't let bad days discourage you!!! Not every day is going to be perfect. Remember, this is a learning process. Realize that there will be great days and not-so-great days. When things don't go so well one day, look at what went wrong, and try to learn from it. Try to find a different way to handle the situation, whatever it may be, or make notes to yourself not to repeat a mistake. Then, let it go, and realize that tomorrow is a new day and a chance to start all over again.

HAPPY SUBBING!!